**Ciaran O'Driscoll**

# The Speaking Trees

SurVision Books

First published in 2018 by
SurVision Books
Dublin, Ireland
www.survisionmagazine.com

Copyright © Ciaran O'Driscoll, 2018

Design © SurVision Books, 2018

ISBN: 978-1-9995903-1-4

This book is in copyright. No part of this publication may be reproduced, stored in a retrieval system or transmitted in any form or by any means without the prior permission in writing from the publisher.

*Acknowledgements*

Grateful acknowledgement is made to the editors of the following, in which a number of these poems originally appeared:

*Cyphers, The Enchanting Verses* (India), *The Irish Times, Molossus, Outburst,* and *SurVision.* Some of these poems have previously appeared in Ciaran O'Driscoll's chapbook, *Surreal Man* (Pighog Press, Brighton, UK, 2006), in his collection entitled *Life Monitor* (Three Spires Press, Cork, Ireland, 2009), and in *Poems of the Decade: An Anthology of the Forward Books of Poetry* (Faber & Faber, 2015).

CONTENTS

Magritte     4
As Regards the Dark     5
The Lost Jockey     6
Please Hold     8
Gluttony     10
Carol     12
Fairies     13
Angel Hour     14
Dead Recital     16
Budapest Quartet     18
An Interview with Ivan     20
Man in Field Talking to Cows     22
Head     24
Old Possum's Stray     26
The Speaking Trees     28
Dogbark Metaphysics     30
Once upon October     31
Frost on a Snowy Evening     32

## Magritte

I am a man in a black bowler hat,
showing my back to the world.
If I turn, an apple blocks my face.

My first glimpse of art was in a churchyard,
so close is it to death.
I listened to the silence of that place.

Sometimes, laid out, she elevates behind me
as I walk the towpath.
Stiff-necked, I do not look around.

My art has no laws of gravity,
but a woman's chestnut hair falls to the ground
and bowler-hatted men are falling rain.

I have seen boulders floating in the sky,
and every day a cloud comes in my door.
Baguettes, instead of clouds, go drifting by.

In woods, between the horse's head and rider,
a vista slips, slim as the trunk of a tree.
What's visible hides what's also visible.

The sea is one with what is not the sea.

## As Regards the Dark

Tell me now as regards the dark.
How far did you go into it?
I didn't go too far in. Far enough.
Further than I bargained for, into the dark.

Have you plans to return into the dark?
I have plans not to return there,
insofar as one is able to plan
not to return into the dark.

And tell me this as regards the dark,
what did you find when you went
not too far but far enough,
further than you bargained for, into the dark?

What I found when I went into the dark
further than I bargained for
and far enough to make me
have plans, insofar as I'm able,

never to return to it
though I didn't go too far in,
was something darker than I bargained for
and that was dark enough.

**The Lost Jockey**

I suppose I always knew, deep down,
that some day it would come to this,
and I would return to the question
posed by that fellow Magritte;
to Chlotho, Lachesis and Atropos,
and snake-haired goddesses,
the Furies or the Fates
or whoever it is they are
who are in hot pursuit.
And when such an event occurs,
erupting on the ordinary scene,
there's always someone watching
from behind a crimson curtain,
who has seen it and says nothing,
only to suffer, thirty years on,
a kind of falling apart.
In the Lowlands they call it the KZ Syndrome
when the truth sprouts from the brain's spindles,
ridiculous but no longer containable.
Was it that he caught my eye
as he galloped past in flight
from those Invisibles,
his face that of an ill-starred child
hidden in the attic for fear of visitors?
There has been far too much geometry
in these parts, the regime
has been far too regular,
and begged a madness to break out,
a thundering of hooves along the drives.

Someone is not in his proper place.
Something is not quite right.
A forest felled and turned
is breaking into leaf.

**Please Hold**


This is the future, my wife says.
We are already there, and it's the same
as the present. Your future, here, she says.
And I'm talking to a robot on the phone.
The robot is giving me countless options,
none of which answer to my needs.
Wonderful, says the robot
when I give him my telephone number.
And Great, says the robot
when I give him my account number.
I have a wonderful telephone number
and a great account number,
but I can find nothing to meet my needs
on the telephone, and into my account
(which is really the robot's account)
goes money, my money, to pay for nothing.
I'm paying a robot for doing nothing.
This call is free of charge, says the robot.
Yes but I'm paying for it, I shout,
out of my wonderful account
into my great telephone bill.
Wonderful, says the robot.
And my wife says, This is the future.
I'm sorry, I don't understand, says the robot.
Please say Yes or No.
Or you can say Repeat or Menu.
You can say Yes, No, Repeat or Menu,
Or you can say Agent if you'd like to talk
to someone real, who is just as robotic.

I scream Agent! and am cut off,
and my wife says, This is the future.
We are already there and it's the same
as the present. Your future, here, she says.
And I'm talking to a robot on the phone,
and he is giving me no options
in the guise of countless alternatives.
We appreciate your patience. Please hold.
Eine Kleine Nachtmusik. Please hold.
Eine Kleine Nachtmusik. Please hold.
Eine fucking Kleine Nachtmusik.
And the robot transfers me to himself.
Your call is important to us, he says.
And my translator says, This means
your call is not important to them.
And my wife says, This is the future.
And my translator says, Please hold
means that, for all your accomplishments,
the only way you can now meet your needs
is by looting. Wonderful, says the robot

Please hold. Please grow old. Please grow cold.
Please do what you're told. Grow old. Grow cold.
This is the future. Please hold.

**Gluttony**

The people I watch in my travels trail
heavier shadows than they did before,
shadows as heavy as a Christmas cake
with eggs and suet, spices, whiskey and porter,
heavy as the plum pudding I was once
served at an Italian summer lunch
while someone hosed the ground around the table.
Surely it's gluttony's repeated weight
has slowed these formerly fast shadows?
And now I see among them my own shadow,
fattened by the truth that dawns with age,
a ripe feast for the jaws of creeping death.
And poetry seems unwilling to let a poet
so heavy inside its portals of ice,
refuses to be the icing on a cake
piped with festivity's legion of names
now that each day is a feast. Waving goodbye
to the spaced-out banquets of the Christian year,
senescent revellers trundle their shadows
from bloat to binge, their vows of exercise
take them no further than the nearest bench
at the edge of the lake, where a mallard chick
has strayed from its mother and mates and goes
piping in a panic between two jetties,
back and forth, back and forth. Meanwhile the poet,
his shadow replete with Austrian pastries,
his heart forty-five per cent efficient,
a vegetation spreading to make a lawn

at his aorta's portal, is getting spooked
by the lost duckling's distress signal, wants
it to stop, wants all the piping to stop.

**Carol**

In the presence of the presence
that's been present all along,
some things are terribly right
and some are terribly wrong.

Some things are terribly clear
and some are still subliminal.
They're singing the same old song
from the new Higgs Boson Hymnal.

The octopus dreams of the fisherman's wife.
The sea is a gift and an affliction.
The trees outside my window
are bare without exception.

The dishwasher's gulping water.
The world is brought to its knees.
A full moon has shown up among
branches' intricacies.

**Fairies**
*(Skocjan, Slovenia)*

I have a constant sense that many more
are present here than meet the eye. And when
I turn as if addressed, from near or far,
by name or with the same effect, these beings,
elusive as water to the fist, have left
only a shade of scent or the unfinished
flourishes of signatures in clefts
under the shifting canyons of the sky.

At three in the morning I got up to greet
the water sprites of the river known as River –
wreaker of time's slow damages beneath
the surface of the Karst. I listened to
a palaver of steady demolition
and was smitten by love of the fairies,
losing the good sleep of my golden years
to be reborn in poems and puberty.

I peer into the sinkhole by the village,
see that its sides are covered in
wild flowers and foliage of sapling shoots.
The altar in the church of St. Canzian
trembles above the abyss on a bridge of rock.
A perpetual procession of clouds and ghosts
moves on the rush of the late August wind.
I keep my counsel, eat my breakfast toast.

## Angel Hour

This morning I thought of the angels
I saw in a pre-dinner catnap
some years ago in Istria
and the tremendous crack
of thunder that same day
in a village where we lunched
on our way back to the coast.
I remember how they stood
in rank with their backs to me
on a road of golden clouds
that climbed into the sky
from our holiday bedroom.
Luminous, light as whispers,
I fancy they appeared
at the equidistant point
between lunch and dinner,
and wonder was that the point
of fasting in the old
church – vision's possibility,
the feats of saints and martyrs,
the heights of Alvernia,
the desert and the voice
that cried in the wilderness?
The dry thunderclap
started me from my soup:
what I'd read about the war
came to mind though it never got
to the bistro we sat outside
on the borgo's single street.

I had ordered a second glass
of Pinot Grigio when *bang!*
a mortar shell behind me
blasted the afternoon.
But everything was OK,
the thunder merely a warning –
*two glasses are enough –*
and then the angels showed
in the stretch of abstinence
before the night's renewal
of appetite and glut.

**Dead Recital**


Reading in a cafe whose name I can't pronounce
I had two translators and an audience of four
And the four audience were poets and they were dead
And I don't know when they had first become defunct
But there was no doubt about it: I recognised
The condition which is generally known as death,
A state of no longer being alive that befalls
A creature who for a time has lived. The poets sat
Well spread apart in the small auditorium,
Upright or crouched, listening as only the dead
Can listen. One held his chin between finger and thumb
In the accepted critically-thinking pose,
Another's head was falling slowly towards
His arms folded on a table, falling for years
Like a heavy bathtub through a bathroom's dry-rot floor.
I struggled against these stern devotees of death,
Words coming from my mouth alive at first and then
Dying somewhere between me and my patrons,
And the more I spoke the nearer death approached me,
Coming right up, almost to the tip of my tongue,
And I battled with the Angel who could induct me
Into a fellowship of poets dumbed and done
By the blunt-force trauma of indifference.
I marvelled how these bards, the unlistening dead,
Came to be corpsified, arrived at being departed,
How they managed without trying to spread death around,
How skilled they were at rolling out unmindfulness,
How little they had to learn now that they had passed on!
And I wondered who it was had taken their lives away

Because they *must* have been alive once, nothing dies
That has not been alive, and poetry is the life
Of poets, the visceral shiver of delight it brings
The basis of their being. And did it happen that
each one of them, while browsing nonchalantly through
a bookshop once, was love-struck by a loveliness
of lines, won over by a spell of stanzas – these
sad victims of some literary apocalypse
now ghost-riding its ego-servile aftermath?

## Budapest Quartet

1.

A woman half my height in a laneway's entrance
smoking a cigarette, face drained of dreams.

And the man we asked for directions said
I perfectly understand my own English.

Only the brown boy slumped over a book
and his plastic cup revealed my whereabouts.

2.

I sit where the Danube understates its passing
and spring's new leaves are hard to say. And said
before so often, why again? But then
why not another turn about, to go
merry and down, and once more down and merry
in the hard-said spring? Don't worry that they think
you have wasted your days, those philistines:
a splash of green that hangs in air on the river's
opposite bank is no small thing; unheeded
it grows among the lives and it will be
again and find an open eye and they
will take it to their hearts eventually.

3.

It is not fortuitous that I introduce
the Horsemen at this stage, for there they were
on Hero Square, flexing their destinies:
to be is to go, to gallop in all
directions. Otherwise they would have been
the men who sit each day outside my grocer's
shooting the breeze. And nobody is more
shiftless than a Magyar going nowhere,
competing with the weather forecaster,
passing the time of day's litotes.
But how those heroes passed time galloping
in their mustachioed magnificence,
demanding blood not bread, putting a world
of fear together! And the veins that throbbed
in their horses' necks and thighs! I can still
hear the clattering of their hooves at night,
you could say they are always on my shoulder.

4.

A taximan tells us taximan jokes,
gesticulates at the lights. If you can't
say green, take it home with you. Don't throw stones
at heroes or they'll bounce and hit you back.
These guys can do without you forever,
unbending as a lover on the chill
with the square jaw you cannot climb when she
shows you her North Face. But let it be clear
that I am more important than you, Magyars:
this may on the face of it seem unlikely,
but you are dead and I still look for answers.

**An Interview with Ivan**


(The shadow of the dial of day
moves across a Moscow square
as a group of sightseers gather
at a fountain and sculpture
erected to Ivan the Terrible.)

*Ivan, were you truly terrible?*
*Did you really make such a mess*
*or was it all bad press?*

*It's the level of people's denseness*
*that's truly terrible*, says
Ivan waiting for his breakfast,
hoping for marmalade on toast.

I ask him the poet Paddy Bushe's
question: *What distinguishes*
*a sonnet from a massacre?*
He smiles. *It simply comes to number:*
*a thousand prisoners in rows*
*above their self-dug graves,*
*and fourteen lines of pentameter.*

Ivan regards the weather
from his dining room windows.
*It's like me, terrible,* he says,
and calls for wellingtons, to wade

through rivers of innocent blood.
(A boy is dropping leaves
in the fountain. His sister chases doves.)

**Man in Field Talking to Cows**


Man in field talking to cows
in the early morning, we're skirting you
on a wide berth of motorway, but for all
we accomplish in the end, for all we do,
we might as well be in a field like you
talking to cows. And it's no bad call
to be out and about and standing in a field
at the break of day and talking to cows,
to be able to talk to them, have the know-how.
And it would be an even greater feat
if the cows were to talk back, as well they might,
and for a proper parley to ensue,
with white mist blanketing the ground
while we are airport-bound
skirting your field in a wide arc
through the dissipating dark.

We're going to Italy to take the air
in hinterlands hill-towned and singular,
where livestock's scarcely sighted out on grass
nor man in meadow glimpsed, talking to cows,
but grape-growers are known to trust in song
for optimal results, and one morning
a neighboring recital rose to keep
a pair of frazzled travellers from sleep,
unsure how blessed they were to be alive
and hear a vineyard opera at five.

Are those the spokescattle, the two beside you?
Have you a name for each herd-member? Is
the most serene of them called Molly? Does
the teat-cup kicker go by Briggs, and how
do you talk her back to rights?... But what would I
know about cows? I knew a little once,
now I don't pause to think the juice that lightens
the colour of my morning coffee flows
from biddable beasts like these you put to browse
in pasture on the edge of a motorway.

I wonder who'll travel furthest today,
you or me, man in field talking to cows.

**Head**

There's a head on the water. I see it
every morning and evening as I stand
on the beach's frothy edge – the walrus head
of a healthy human specimen between
me and the motor-driven schooners moored
in mid-harbour, their sails superfluous
and furled; between the open sea
and the cactus-clustered mountains.

Between me on the hissing hem of froth
and the schooners' supernumerary sails,
between the cliffs and the promenade I see
a regular middle-aged humanoid head,
a brine-encompassed brainbox that proceeds
stealthily from my waking to my sleep,
its wet mouth lapped by whiskers, half-closed eyes
rapt in some indecipherable bliss.

A head that has made this incongruous
element its own, a head on its own
that has made the sea its own, a head
that I cannot get out of my own head,
moving without making sense between
the harbour mouth and the holiday apartments,
*de facto* as the cactus plants that rest
snug in their places on the mountain slopes.

I watch it daily from the ocean's edge
shifting without a ripple or a wake
in the lagoon between a reef of boats
and my reluctant water-testing toes,
I see it floating through recurrent dreams –
a king in a country of his own making,
*capo di capi* not to be discounted
in the fortunate isles of imagination.

A cranium building a head of steam
in its unwimpling progress up and down
the smoothness of the surface, unconcerned
by what is happening offshore or on.
This head of heads, no other head's contentment,
content without companion head, ensconced
in isolated mindfulness. A head
to end all heads, the mother of all heads.

**Old Possum's Stray**


Yellow Fog, the tortoiseshell,
licked the evening with her tongue
and open sesame, a song
which had been stowed away till then
in the corners of non-entity
came suddenly to be
and all was up for grabs again
as she climbed down the pergola.

This miracle of Yellow Fog
having proved not at all
of relevance to reality,
life moved ahead and quizzical
was the cat about the creatures
of the air that twitched in hedges
as she marched her self-defined
domain and answered supper's call.

Yellow Fog the tortoiseshell
is not well known except by those
new owners who sustain
her penchant for surprise,
springing for the most part
the very inconvenient sort
by which they step on feline fur
in her moveable sunlit place.

Therefore the tortoiseshell shall not
be glorified too much, and is
like *lonely men in shirtsleeves*
*leaning out of windows,*
their pipe-smoke transient and pungent
as Yellow Fog's auspicious moment
licking the evening with her tongue
to open sesame for song.

## The Speaking Trees
*(Gatwick, 2nd May 2005)*


We have troubles, say the trees, but we don't worry.
We're a green stripe on the edge of a grey airport
after your bad day at the office. We're a shout
in your eye, an outburst of arboreal cheer.
Ours is a different time-scale: we're content
to hold tight here while you rush to and fro.
We haven't too much sympathy for the edgy:
there's something keeps us singing on the edge
of existence or an airport. We offer perspective
by our comportment, which is quite other.
Soon – any moment now – you will lift your head
and the sight of us will put proportion on
the day's troubles, help you become more rooted
in the sense that moving creatures may be so.
We are the leafy Yes in your day of No
endured where speed spins all colours to a grey
community. But we will slow you down
when we enter your head. Your thoughts will stop darting,
though you'll still be able to shake an arm about.
You may wave at us if you like – pretend
you are waving at friends, it could be true.
What's about to happen, when you meet our gaze,
could very properly be called a greeting.
We are the masters of mobility
because we have learned to move while staying put,
and we feel we are ideally placed
here on the rim of vision to supply you
with a sustaining image. We're afraid

you have become deaf to the cheering of trees,
you are out of touch with your branches and leaves.
You could also do with understanding time,
how to behave within it. This is not done well
by searching feverishly among pockets
for your ticket. You have far too many pockets.
Between departure lounge and boarding steps,
we'd love to tell you of those other steppes,
the grasslands of the great indifference.
In a few more seconds, when you notice us,
you'll know that nothing matters much – the state
of the finances, the meltdown at the office,
tailbacks, missed departures, engineering works.
We could say the same thing more starkly in winter
but we feel that you need a touch of colour
in how the message is phrased: something green
catches your eye although it's going nowhere,
and a quality you thought extinct still lives;
in a language fallen out of use, it speaks
of surprises and potentials in yourself,
the strength to let go and find unlikely comfort
in a stand of trees on a grey airport's edge.

Look now – and don't be ashamed to wave at us
as you show your boarding card to the hostess.
When you sit and shut your eyes on all the stress,
you'll fall into our dance of rootedness.

## Dogbark Metaphysics

*A dog barking is just a barking dog.*
*And I wish he'd stop, he's been barking all day.*

There is another way of looking at it,
and this is not a question of quantity,
how many barks will a dog have barked
before expiring, as if bark were a piece
of dog flaking off into nothingness,
nor of how many barks can dance between
a kite and its windsurfer, between
the crescent moon and its evening star,
but rather a question of *dasein*
the *being there* of a dog, barking *I'm here*,
and there's another way of looking at it,
that there should be dog at all,
that there should at all be barking,
that there should be *this this this*
and then *this*, followed by not-this,
that there should be *this* rather than not-this,
and there's still another way of looking at it:
how to unlock the enigma of the *Now*,
Not now, *Now*, *Now*, Not now, *Now*,
the barking of what we cannot hear,
barking of what we cannot see,
the Dog-Lorentz Transformations
of light that has yet to reach us.

**Once upon October**

Drinking with great old characters
in the great old drunken way,
the old thought came to me
*What will I do now that the leaves
are slipping through my letter box
sealed with the red of autumn?*
I drove and passed the signs
of several county borders,
no wife at home to tolerate me
after the tolerance of
that bona fide fellowship.
It was Hallowe'en, the hedges dressed
as harlequins – later the soft
crackle of fireworks in the night
as I hit the doorstep,
a welcoming committee
of hungry cats, and why was my key
not fitting in the lock?
Eventually, there appeared
a beautiful young man
in cut-off jeans, who looked
me thoroughly up and down
as I stood on the threshold
dumbfounded, miaowed upon.
*Interesting,* he purred.
*Why don't you come on in?*
Fireworks crackled softly.
The key eased into the lock.

## Frost on a Snowy Evening

*(i.m. Macdara Woods)*


Snow fell that evening as I was heading home,
and at the woods I knew I should drive on:
my wife would worry, things had to be done
that couldn't be postponed, but all the same
I pulled into a roadside parking place
to see the snow falling among the trees
and covering them. I've lost the poem now
but I remember spending time with it
that evening I stopped by the woods in snow.

I know I must have thought they were too simple
or otherwise had been already said
so I left them and wrote something else instead,
at least it was my own, and a good call
I didn't stay with *lovely, dark and deep,*
even though they were and always will be,
and that's a better way to describe them
than what I wrote – not scared of being too plain
and at the same time getting it spot on
for many winter woods, and one I knew
whose poems were parented in falling snow.

www.ingramcontent.com/pod-product-compliance
Lightning Source LLC
Chambersburg PA
CBHW061315040426
42444CB00010B/2655